D0771275

Published by Doubleday, a division of
Bantam Doubleday Dell Publishing Group, Inc.
666 Fifth Avenue, New York, New York 10103

Doubleday and the portrayal of an anchor with a dolphin
are trademarks of Doubleday, a division of
Bantam Doubleday Dell Publishing Group, Inc.

Library of Congress Cataloging-in-Publication Data
Cook, Brenda.
All about farm animals/by Brenda Cook; illustrated by
Ann Winterbotham.—1st ed. in the U.S.A.
p.   cm.
Includes index.
Summary: An introduction to farm animals and to the basic workings
of a farm.
1. Domestic animals—Juvenile literature.   2. Farm life—Juvenile
literature. [1. Domestic animals.   2. Farm life.]
I. Winterbotham, Ann L., ill.   II. Title.
SF75.5.C66 1989
636'.01—dc19   88-20262
CIP
AC
ISBN 0-385-24821-0 (Trade)
0-385-24822-9 (Library)

FIRST EDITION IN THE UNITED STATES OF AMERICA, 1989

BRENDA COOK

ALL ABOUT FARM ANIMALS

Illustrated by
Ann Winterbotham

DOUBLEDAY
NEW YORK LONDON TORONTO SYDNEY AUCKLAND

Contents

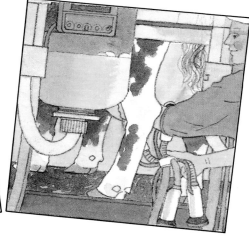

Wake up, farm!

Early in the morning when most of us are asleep in bed, the farmer is already out in the farmyard. The cock is crowing and the cows are coming up to the gate because they know it is time to be milked.

9

Milking time

The farmer keeps cows for their milk. They are milked twice a day—once in the morning and once in the afternoon.

The cows like to come to the milking parlor because they know they will get pellets made of corn to eat. Because they are enjoying the food, they stand quietly while the farmer cleans their udders and attaches the cups of the milking machine to their teats.

The milk is sucked from the teats of each cow along a pipe and into a container. When the milk stops coming, the farmer looks at the containers to see how much milk each cow has given.

The dairy

The milk comes along pipes from the milking parlor into a tank in the dairy.

The tank is like a big refrigerator. When milk comes from a cow it is warm. The refrigerator cools it down and keeps it cold.

When all the cows have been milked, and the cowman has washed down the parlor, the cat gets her drink of milk.

The calves

A cow makes milk to feed her calf, so a cow has to have a calf before she can produce milk for the farmer.

After her calf is born, she will give milk for almost a year, but then she must have another calf before she will give milk again.

The calves drink powdered milk mixed with water. The females are called heifer calves, and the males are called bull calves.

What happens to milk

The milk tanker comes to the farm once a day. The driver connects up a pipe to collect the milk.

The driver calls at several other farms for more milk. When he has a full load, he drives to the milk factory.

After the morning milking the cows go back to the field to eat grass. They will come in again to be milked in the afternoon.

At the factory some of the milk is treated to make it safe for us to drink. Then a machine squirts it into cartons and seals them to keep the milk fresh.

The rest of the milk is made into other dairy food. Butter, cream, cheese, and yogurt are made from milk and there is milk in ice cream and chocolate.

Lambing time

Spring is a busy time on farms which have sheep. This is when the lambs are born. Their mothers are called ewes.

The farmer has brought these ewes inside a barn, so that the lambs can be born where it is warm and dry. Sometimes the farmer gives a few puffs of oxygen to a newborn lamb to help it start breathing.

The lambs struggle to their feet a few minutes after they are born. They soon learn to walk on their wobbly legs and find their way to the ewe's udder where they suck her milk.

For at least two weeks the lambs' only food is their mothers' milk. Then they start to eat grass and grain. The farmer gives this to them a little at a time.

Sometimes a ewe dies and her newborn lamb is left without a mother. When this happens, the lamb has to be fed from a bottle like a baby. The farmer's wife is feeding this lamb in the warm farmhouse kitchen.

Spring babies

Other animals on the farm also have young ones in the spring.

One of the farm cats has a litter of kittens. When they grow up, they will help to keep mice away.

The nanny goat gives more milk than her kids need, so there is some left over for the farmer to sell.

The pony's baby is called a foal. The foal stays very close to its mother, following her wherever she goes.

The hen has been sitting on her eggs for three weeks, keeping them warm and turning them with her feet from time to time. At last the eggs begin to crack and the chicks struggle out.

Sheep and lambs

The lambs go out to the fields with their mothers when they are a few weeks old. They are very frisky, but they come to their mothers when they are called.

There are many wild birds in the fields too. Pheasants and pigeons like to feed on the farmer's crops.

Noisy crows build their nests high up in the trees. Sometimes there are fifty nests in one tree.

The goats

The goats stay near the house. The nanny goat is milked by hand twice a day. Her milk is good to drink, but most of it is made into cheese.

The goats have a dry shed to sleep in at night and to shelter in on days when the weather is bad.

The kids are as playful as the lambs. They chase and butt each other and jump about.

A rainy day

The farm animals look for shelter whenever it starts to rain heavily. Only the ducks enjoy the rain.

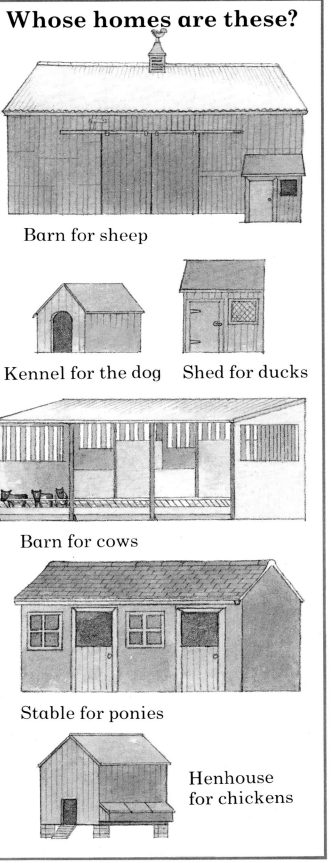

Whose homes are these?

Barn for sheep

Kennel for the dog   Shed for ducks

Barn for cows

Stable for ponies

Henhouse for chickens

Grass-eaters

Sheep, cows, ponies, and geese all eat grass. In
the summer there is plenty of it because the
warm sunshine and the showers of rain make it
grow quickly. The sheep nibble away at the
grass until they have made it very short.

A cow does not nibble grass like a sheep. She wraps her tongue around a bunch of grass and pulls at it. Then she swallows it and the long pieces of grass form into balls in her stomach.

After a while the balls in her stomach start coming back up into the cow's mouth, and she lies down to chew them well before she swallows them again. This is called chewing the cud.

Feeding the hens

Every day the hens have to be fed and their
eggs collected. When the hens are fed, sparrows
and pigeons often come and try to steal some
of the grain. The hens must be locked up safely
in the henhouse at night
in case a fox comes around.

Hens, ducks, and geese are different kinds of poultry. They all lay eggs that are good to eat, but it is usually hen's eggs that we buy.

Hen's egg　　　　**Duck egg**　　　　**Goose egg**

Ducks and geese

Ducks are water birds and they find most of their food in the water. The ducklings follow their mother into the water and are soon swimming around happily.

The farm geese like to be near the pond, but they do not swim on it. They wander about eating weeds and grass. Like the hens, ducks and geese are locked up at night to keep them safe.

Sheep shearing

Early in the summer the farmer collects all the sheep together ready for shearing.

During the cold winter weather the sheep grew thick woolen coats to keep them warm. They do not need all this wool when summer comes.

Each sheep is held firmly while the sheepshearer cuts off its fleece with electric clippers. It is like having a haircut and does not hurt.

The sheepdogs help him to round up the sheep and herd them into a pen near the barns.

The fleece usually comes off in one piece and looks very big when it is spread out. The sheepshearer rolls it up to send it off to be sold.

The sheep look very clean and much smaller after the shearing. Their wool will grow again in time to keep them warm next winter.

The countryside

It is great fun to ride on a pony through the countryside. Many wild animals live there. Can you name the ones in this picture?

In the old days, when there were no vans or tractors, horses and ponies worked on the farm. Today the farmer keeps them for riding.

The pig farm

There are many farms to visit nearby. Some of them keep just one kind of animal. This one is a pig farm. It has hundreds of pigs inside its sheds but no cows or sheep or poultry.

Pigs and piglets

The pigs live inside all the year round. The farmer makes sure each one gets the right amount of food, such as grains, fish meal, and skimmed milk.

A mother pig is called a sow. When it is time for her to have her piglets she is moved to a farrowing pen. A sow usually has between ten and fourteen piglets at a time.

Young piglets must not get cold, so the farmer hangs an infrared lamp over their pen. They sleep under the warm light when they are not feeding from their mother.

Tell this story

If we are out in the countryside, we can help to keep farm animals safe and out of trouble by making sure that farm gates are shut.

Looking after farm animals

The farrier comes to the farm when the ponies need new shoes. They have shoes made of iron to protect their hooves from hard ground.

The farrier has measured the hooves and knows what size shoes to bring. He nails on the shoes, but it does not hurt the pony.

Just as people have to have their nails cut, so cows and sheep have to have their hooves trimmed. The farmer often does this job himself.

When animals are hurt or ill, the farmer sends for a vet. On this visit the vet is giving a sheep an injection.

The vet uses a stethoscope to examine this cow, while the farmer strokes the cow's head to keep it calm.

Harvesting

Early in the fall, after the warm summer sun has ripened the grain, the farmer uses a combine harvester to cut the wheat.

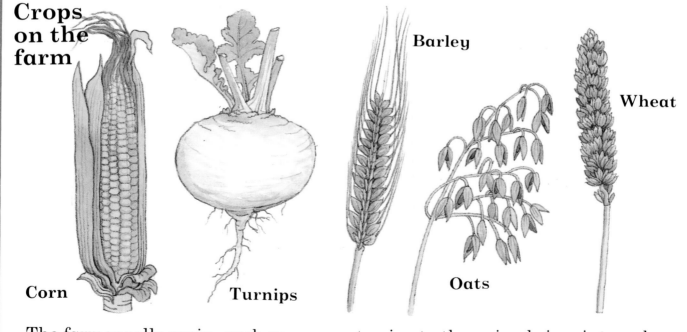

Crops on the farm

Corn

Turnips

Barley

Oats

Wheat

The farmer sells grain, such as wheat, barley, and oats, to be made into pellets of animal food. The farmer buys some of these pellets to give to the animals in winter when the grass does not grow. To provide more winter food, the farmer also grows turnips and corn.

The harvester strips the grain from the plants and leaves behind the stalks. The stalks are rolled into big bales of straw. The farmer uses some of this to provide bedding for all the animals.

In the fall there are plowing matches. Many people come to see the big horses and to watch how plowing was done in the old days.

Then there were no tractors and heavy horses pulled all the machines on the farm. The shire horse is one of the largest horses in the world.

Winter

When winter comes, the farmer brings the cows and sheep inside the barns. He likes to have them under cover before the snow is really thick.

The sheep and cows stay indoors until the snow has gone. While they are inside they have to be fed every day. Now is the time when the farmer uses his store of winter feed. He gives them hay and silage, made from grass grown earlier in the year, as well as grain pellets.

Seasons

As they watch the snow fall, the farmer and his family think about the seasons that have gone.

Spring

Summer

Fall

Winter

Now it is winter and the fields are cold and bare, but the family look forward to the next spring and to another busy year on the farm.